Stephen Curry: The Story of One of the Best Basketball Shooters and Point Guards of All Time

Stephen Curry: The Story of One of the Best Basketball
Shooters and Point Guards of All Time

Copyright © 2019 James Madison

Table of Contents

Chapter 1:

Pre-NBA

Stephen Curry is an American basketball player for the Golden State Warriors who is often regarded by many as one of the greatest shooters in NBA history. He was born on March 14th, 1988 in Akron, Ohio, and is the son of former NBA player Dell Curry. To gain a true idea and understanding of his accomplishments in his NBA career it's important to take a look into his journey prior to entering the NBA.

Steph grew up in Charlotte, North Carolina where his

first pick and selected Dell Curry. He played ten official seasons with the Charlotte Hornets and is currently the Hornets franchise leader in points scored with 9,839 points.

Shortly after the families move to North Carolina, they welcomed the birth of Stephen's younger brother, Seth, and his younger sister Sydel. Stephen's younger brother Seth also followed in his father's footsteps and currently plays for the Portland Trail Blazers. Although the family was heavily involved in sports, they held a high priority on academics and faith and made sure the kids didn't feel pressured to follow in their father's footsteps.

While his dad was traveling and playing basketball, Steph's mom took on the role to strictly discipline the kids and ensure they have a proper understanding of respect and responsibility. Steph's mom was so strict that one day she did not allow him to go to practice because he had forgotten to wash the dishes at home. These basic disciplines is what made Steph work relentlessly on his shooting. The moment Steph stepped on the court, it was obvious he was light years ahead of the competition. Although smaller than most of his peers he was draining shoots from deep behind the three-point line which helped his team dominate the competition. As easy as he makes the game look, his road to greatness has not been as smooth as you might imagine.

As a high school sophomore Steph stood at 5'6 and weighed only 125 pounds. Lacking height and strength he tended to shoot the ball straight from his waist. His father told him that if he wanted to play at the collegiate level he would have to make a serious adjustment to his shot in order to make it harder for defenders to block. The following summer Steph worked relentlessly on his shot to bring it high above his head. He was up early in the mornings and stayed late into the night practicing his shots while other kids were sleeping in and playing video games. His brother Seth recalls that it was difficult for him to watch how hard Steph worked on his shot late into the night and how frustrated Steph would get at himself. He often thought about giving up because how hard he struggled to adjust his shot. He pushed himself beyond his frustrations to the point where he mastered his shot and shooting the basketball became second nature to him.

With his newly remastered shot, Steph averaged just

under 20 points per game in his junior season of high school. Although an improvement from the previous season, he would have to continue to get better in order to make his name stand out. Steph knew early on that he wanted to play for a big-time school such as Duke, NC State, Carolina or Wake Forest. He wanted to play for a team where he would have the chance to play against elite competition. Unfortunately, those schools never ended up recruiting him or showing any signs of interest. Most recruiters said that Steph was too small to play at the next level and make any serious impact in games. The negativity and skeptics only fueled Steph to work even harder on his game. His relentless work ethic eventually landed him a basketball scholarship in 2008 to Davidson College located just nineteen miles north of Charlotte.

Chapter 2:

Collegiate Career – Freshman Year

Although a lesser known school in terms of basketball accolades, Davidson College molded Stephen Curry into the superstar he is today. While other coaches were criticizing Steph's size and playing potential, coach McKillop saw a future star in the making. Davidson College heavily recruited Steph since the tenth grade and head coach Bob McKillop spotted Steph's natural talent very early on. Coach McKillop was so confident about Steph's skills that he praised him at a Davidson alumni event before Steph even played his first game for the Wildcats.

Despite coach McKillops confidence in Steph, he had a sloppy first game. In his very first collegiate debut against Eastern Michigan in the 2006-2007 season, Steph had 15 points along with 13 turnovers. He almost had just as many turnovers as he did points. Steph was not used to the new speed and talent level of his veteran competitors. He would have to make a serious effort and change to his game in order to become a better player and compete at the collegiate level. Despite his 9 turnovers in the first half of the game, coach McKillop kept Steph in the second half of the game. Steph sunk two deep three-pointers in the third and fourth quarter to help the Wildcats seal 81-77 victory over Eastern Michigan. Although Steph received widespread criticism due to his many turnovers in his first game, he kept his head up and made a statement in his second game against the University of Michigan.

In his second game against the University of Michigan Wolverines, Steph dropped 32 points, 9 rebounds and 4 assists. A massive improvement over his first game and a testament to this will and dedication to improving not only his game but the dynamic of his team. Steph shot 6-for-

13 to score the 17 first-half points and went 4-for-9 from the three-point line. The much more experienced and heavily favored Wolverines went on to beat the Wildcats 78-68, but it became apparent to critics and fans that Steph Curry was going to be a serious player.

During the month of November of their opening season, the Wildcats crushed smaller teams like Central Connecticut State and Illinois Chicago, but began to struggle against teams such Missouri in the Big 12 and Duke in the ACC. Duke beat the Wildcats 75-47 and coach McKillop quickly took notice that Steph struggled with turnovers against major programs. It would be something that Steph would have to seriously improve on if he planned to go to the NBA.

Following the Wildcats loss to Duke, they went on to win 22 out of their final 23 regular season games with their only loss coming from a close 81-74 game to Appalachian State. Their impressive record secured them the number one ranking in the Southern Conference for the 2006-2007 season. It was no doubt the reason for the teams massive improvement over the previous season was directly due to the impact made my Steph. He went on to average 21.5 points, 4.6 rebounds and 2.8 assists per game in his freshman year. He was also the leading scorer in the Southern Conference with a total of 730 points and a three-point shooting average of 40.8 percent. Steph also went on the break the 3-point record in a single season with 113th threes and Davidson's freshman scoring record of 502 points in a single season. He was the second leading among freshman in scoring following Kevin Durant who averaged 25.8 points per game and is now his teammate on the Golden State Warriors. His basketball accolades and reputation for being a sharp three-point shooter were quickly stacking up. It made fans and critics wonder how this skinny talented point guard slipped through the hands of some of the more established basketball powerhouses.

Steph's sharp shooting helped Davidson secure a 29-5 overall record and a 17-1 conference record. Alongside that, the Wildcats won a Southern Conference regular season title and stepped into the NCAA tournament as a 13th seed to face off with a 4th seed Maryland. The much more experienced Maryland Terrapins ended up winning the game

82-70 despite Steph's impressive 30-point performance. At the end of his freshman year, Steph racked up the following awards below.

- Southern Conference Freshman of the Year
- SoCon Tournament MVP
- SoCon All-tournament team
- All-freshman team
- First team All-SoCon

To say Steph had a successful freshman year would be a serious understatement. His coaches, fans and critics were not only impressed but started to see a potential NBA superstar in the making.

Chapter 3: Collegiate Career

Sophomore Year

By the beginning of his sophomore season Steph had grown an additional 2 inches from 6'1 to 6'3. His second season started off much like his first, against opponents who out of his conference. In the months of November and December in the 2007-2008 season the Wildcats faced North Carolina, Western Michigan, North Carolina Central, Duke, Charlotte, USCLA and North Carolina State. The only game that the Wildcats won against a team who was out of their conference was against North Carolina Central who they blew out 98-50. Big teams out of their conference proved to be a challenge yet again this year. But this season would be very different, not only for Steph but for the Wildcats as well.

The Wildcats were not just beating teams in their conference, they were absolutely dismantling and embarrassing them. Their first game of the season set the tone that would follow for the rest of the 2007-2008 season. They absolutely destroyed Emory 120-56 in their season opener in the Belk Arena. Sports analysts, NBA scouts and critics all had their eye on Curry.

At the end of his sophomore season Steph once again led the Southern Conference in scoring. He averaged 25.9 points, 4.6 rebounds and 2.9 assists per game. His three-point shooting percentage improved from 40.8% the previous season to 43.9%. His field goal percentage went up by 2% from 46.3% the previous season to 48.3%. Many people believe his improvements came due to switching his position to a shooting guard from a point guard the previous season. Regardless of the fact, he had a stellar improvement over his freshman year. His improvement was a testament that he was focused on proving everyone wrong who previously doubted his talent and his ability to become a dominant guard. Unbeknownst to many, Curry had a torn ligament in his left wrist in the beginning of the season which he would later need surgery for. He decided to play through his injury and pain for all 36-regular season games and wait until after the season was over to get surgery. An absolute warrior, no pun intended. Steph led the Wildcats to a 26-6 regular season record, and a 20-0 conference record. His sharp shooting and exceptional leadership as a guard helped lead Davidson to another NCAA tournament bid. Little did Steph know, this tournament would be an experience he would never forget.

The Wildcats first NCAA tournament game was against a seventh-seed Gonzaga on Friday March 21, 2008. The first half of the game stayed very tight between the two teams. Gonzaga would go on to take their biggest lead 28-17 midway through the first half. Towards the end of the first half, Jason Richards of the Wildcats managed to close the gap by getting Gonzaga into foul trouble and sinking 4 free throws. The score at the end of the first half was 41-36 with Gonzaga in the lead. Steph had been quite in the first half sinking only 2 threes and 2 mid-range jumpers. In the second half of the game Steph started to catch fire and the course of the game started to shift. In the first 20 seconds of the second half Steph came off a nice pick and roll and sunk a 3-pointer from the perimeter to close the gap in the score to 41-39. Another minute later after Gonzaga's Steven Gray made a 3 pointer, Curry answered back with a 3 pointer of his own to keep the game tight. The rest of the game was an all-out shooting war. With 9:47 remaining in the game, Steph sunk another 3-pointer to tie the game 62-62. It was obvious that neither team wanted to lose and Steph would have to bring his best shooting out in order to help the Wildcats win. At the 1:47 mark with the Wildcats up 74-72, Gonzaga's Jeremy Pargo made a layup to tie the game 74-74. At this point in the game the crowd was on their feet. As the Wildcats began to dribble up the court the building was rumbling with excitement. After a missed 3-pointer by Paulhus Gosselin and the clock winding down, Andrew Lovedale got the offensive rebound and kicked the ball out to Curry who sunk a big 3-pointer to put the Wildcats up 77-74. After Curry sunk the 3-pointer the announcer yelled **"Are you kidding me?",** as the crowd fired up. Gonzaga failed to make a comeback after Curry's 3-pointer and the Wildcats went on to win the game 82-76. Steph ended the game with 40 points on an 8-for-10 from the 3-point line. He absolutely carried the Wildcats to win the game dropping 30 of his 40 points in the second half.

Two days following their win over seventh-seed Gonzaga, Curry and the Wildcats faced a second seed Georgetown in the second round of the NCAA tournament. Coming off a huge performance and now facing a much tougher team, it was crucial for Steph to prove his talent. Steph had a slow start to the game and looked very tired during the first half while getting swarmed by Georgetown's defense any time he touched the ball. Georgetown knew that if they left him open for even a second, he would be a serious threat. Georgetown's aggressive defense managed to hold Steph to measly 5 points in the first half and at halftime they held the lead 38-27.

Steph would have to have another mind-blowing second half performance like he did against Gonzaga in order to stand a chance of beating Georgetown. After missing his first 3 shots in the second half, Steph sunk a 3-pointer and once again started sinking shots left and right. Knowing that Georgetown would be all over him anytime he touched the ball around the perimeter, Steph started looking for contact on his shots. As a result he ended up getting to the free throw line 10 times. He would go on to make 9 out of his 10 free throws and 25 of his 30 points all came in the second half of the game. The Wildcats would end up closing a 17-point second half deficit and force Georgetown to 20 turnovers to eventually end up winning the game 74-70. The Wildcats had stunned a second seed Georgetown and advanced to the next round of the NCAA tournament.

Their next opponent was a third-seeded Wisconsin, which would end up being a very close game with the score tied 36-36 at halftime. Both teams played an extremely physical first half, but Curry once again shined in the second half of the game to help secure another win for the Wildcats. Steph would end up outscoring the whole Wisconsin

Badgers team by himself in the second half, 22-20. He finished the game with 33 points and Davidson won the game 73-56 to advance to the Elite 8. Steph's 33-point performance helped him join an elite club of players such Clyde Lovellete of Kansas, Jerry Chambers of Utah and Glen Robinson of Purdue as the only players to score over 30 points in their first four NCA tournament games.

The Wildcats next opponent were the Kansas Jayhawks, who were an extremely physical team and very aware of Steph's sharp shooting ability. It was such a tough and close game that both teams didn't even break double digits points until halfway into the first half of the game. At halftime the score was 30-28 with the Jayhawks in the lead. The second half continued to be extremely close with the lead never going above 6 points. With 54 seconds left to go in the game and the Jayhawks up 59-54, Steph made a 3 pointer and Davidson immediately took a 30 second timeout following his shot. The Wildcats were down only 2 points now 59-57. Following the Wildcats timeout, the Jayhawks wound down the clock to 36 seconds and called a timeout. After the timeout at the 19 second mark

Sherron Collins of the Jayhawks shot a 3 pointer and missed and Davidson quickly scooped up the defensive rebound and called a full timeout.

The Wildcats ran a quick play which got Jason Richards open for a three-pointer to try and win the game but unfortunately, he missed the shot and they Jayhawks ended up winning the game 59-57. Had Curry taken the last shot the outcome of the game might have been completely different. Curry had an amazing game with 25 points on a 9-of-25 shooting and was named the Most Outstanding Player of the Midwest Regional. Although disappointed in the loss, Curry was happy with how hard his team fought. "We made history for our school, "Curry said. "Not a lot of people expected a lot from us, so I'm proud of what we have accomplished, but it hurts a lot to have been this close to the Final Four".

Chapter 4: Collegiate Career

Junior Year

Following the Wildcats loss to the Kansas Jayhawks, many fans and critics wondered whether Curry would declare for the NBA draft or stay for one more season to try and bring Davidson a NCAA title. After much consideration Steph decided to stay one more year at Davidson and further develop himself as a point guard in order to have a better chance of being a top draft prospect. At this point in his collegiate career many people considered him one of the top college basketball point guards in the country. One thing was for certain, this season would be one that college fans would never forget.

Curry and the Wildcats had a hot start to their 2008-2009 season, beating teams they previously struggled against out of their conference. They managed to beat Winthrop in the Big South, Florida Atlantic in the Sun Belt, Loyola in the MACC, North Carolina State in the ACC, and West Virginia in the Big East. In their third game of the season against Oklahoma, Steph would go on to have a career high 44 points even though the Wildcats ended up losing 82-78. It was evident that his game was not only improving, but he was transforming the very nature of the game. He became a serious threat to teams around the perimeter and many coaches began to realize how effectively a team can play if they have sharp-shooting players behind the arc.

The Wildcats ended 1st in the Southern Conference with an 18-2 record and had an overall record of 27-8 in the 2008-2009 season. On February 28, 2009 Curry would go on to become Davidson's all-time leading scorer with 2,488 career points putting the previous school leader John Gerdy in second place. He averaged 28.6 points, 4.4 rebounds and 5.6 assists per game. By the end of his junior season he managed to have 2,635 point, leaving his mark in the record books of Davidson. The Wildcats would go on to win the Southern Conference regular season championship in the South Division and face Appalachian State in the quarter-finals of the Southern Conference Tournament. Curry had a phenomenal performance scoring 43 points and leading the Wildcats to an 84-68 win over Appalachian State.

In the semi-finals of the Southern Conference tournament, the Wildcats faced the College of Charleston. This would prove to be a tough game for Steph. Despite a solid 20-point performance by Steph, the Wildcats ended up losing the game 52-59. Although valiant efforts were made from coach Bob McKillop and coach Bobby Cremins from Charleston, the Wildcats were unsuccessful in securing a NCAA tournament bid. They would not be able to compete in the NCAA tournament this year and Curry and the Wildcats were very disappointed because they knew how far they could go in the tournament.

Although they were not able to receive a bid in the NCAA tournament this year, the Wildcats received a 6th seed in the 2009 National Invitation Tournament. Even though it wasn't the tournament they wished to play in, it was still a chance for them to prove they were a top tier team. Curry loved to compete and he knew this tournament would most likely be his last time playing at the collegiate level so he was ready and excited to play. In their first game of the 2009 National Invitation Tournament the Wildcats faced third seed South Carolina. Curry poured in 32 points and led the Wildcats to a 70-63 victory over the South Carolina Gamecocks. Curry's next game against the Saint Mary's Gaels would unfortunately the last game of his college career. Davidson ended up losing the game 80-68 and were out of the National Invitation Tournament. Curry ended the game with 26 points, 9 rebounds and 5 assists. Although a disappointing loss, Curry and the Wildcats had an incredible season filled with challenges and special moments they would never forget. At the end of the season Curry was the NCAA leading scorer and was named first team All-American. He had solidified himself as a top point guard and was now fully ready to enter the NBA draft.

Chapter 5:

NBA Draft 2009 and First Season

There was much speculation and uncertainty as to which team would end up selecting a point guard with Curry's skillset. However, there was one team that had their eye on him ever since his sophomore season with Davidson. "And with the seventh overall pick in the 2009 NBA draft the Golden State Warriors select Stephen Curry from Davidson College". The Warriors could not have predicted that their pick would end up changing the very core of their franchise and the way the three-point shot is used in the

NBA. On October 28th 2009, Steph would suit up against the Houston Rockets to make his NBA debut. He played for a total of 35 minutes and racked up 14 points, 7 assists and 4 steals. The Houston Rockets ended up winning the game 108-107 but Steph proved to fans and critics that he could compete at the next level. He was a quick and exciting point guard to watch and the rest of the season he continued to improve his game and make use of his sharp shooting behind the arc.

Steph said that one of the biggest surprises was how much fans get into the game when you're playing at home. He was also shocked that the crowd could help players perform better and shift the momentum of the game. In his first NBA season Steph averaged 17.5 points, 4.5 rebounds, and 5.9 assists per game. His stellar performance in the second half of the season made him a top contender for rookie of year. That year the rookie of the year award was given to Tyreke Evans from the Sacramento Kings and Curry was the runner up. In his first NBA season Curry played 80 games, 77 of which he started in. He also racked up 12 double-doubles and 1 triple double. Although the

Warriors had a record of 26-56 in the 2009-2010 season, Curry was making huge strides as player and leader of the team. One exciting stat that stands out from the rest from his rookie season is that he finished his rookie season with 166 threes made, which were the most ever made by any rookie in NBA history. It set the tone for the kind of sharpshooting point guard he would become in the coming years of his career.

Chapter 6: 2010-2011 Season

(The Transformation)

The 2010-2011 season was a season full of transformation for not only Curry, but for the whole Golden State Warriors organization. The team acquired All-Star forward and center David Lee in a deal with the New York Knicks in exchange for Kelenna Azubuike, Anthony Randolph, Ronny Turiaf and a 2012 second round draft pick. David Lee was a solid addition to the Warriors franchise averaging 20.2 points, 11.7 rebounds and 3.6 assists per game. The Warriors team was also sold to an investor group owned by Kleiner Perkin Caufield & Byers managing partner Joe Lacob and Mandalay Entertainment Group Chairman Peter Guber for $450 million. Considering the kind of powerhouse team the Warrior are today, it's safe to say that the investor purchased them at a bargain. The Warriors also hired head coach Keith Smart to help with changing the dynamic of the franchise around. With the new ownership, new players and staff, and new a logo, the Warriors were well on their way to becoming a powerful team.

In their 2010-2011 season opener against the Houston Rockets, Curry had a double-double consisting of 25 points and 11 assists to lead the Warriors to a 132-128 win. That game set the tone for the rest of the season and the new Warriors organization was going to make a massive impact on the NBA. Curry and his right-hand man Monta Ellis were an exciting duo in the backcourt and managed to play extremely well of each other. Ellis led the Warriors team in scoring that season averaging 24.1 points, 3.5 rebounds and 5.3 assists per game. That season he helped speed up the pace of Curry's game as he was considered by many as one of the fastest guards in the NBA.

In his second NBA season Curry averaged 18.6 points, 3.9 rebounds and 5.8 assists per game. He played a total of 74 games that season and experienced multiple sprains on his right ankle that caused him to miss some games. Regardless of his ankle injury, Steph continued to improve his game that season and increased his 3-point shooting percentage from 46.2% the previous season to 48%. He was essentially making every other three-pointer he took. Curry was quickly becoming a serious threat to teams just like he did when he was with the Wildcats.

On March 11, 2011 the Warriors would go on to set a franchise record for most combined three-pointers made in a single game. They drained 21 three-pointers in a 123-120 overtime win against the Magic. It was becoming evident that the Warriors were changing their style of play to rely more heavily on the use of three pointers. Unfortunately, the Warriors would fail to make the playoffs that season, but things were slowly improving for them with Curry on the roster. They managed to improve their record over the previous season from 26-56 to 36-46. They finished 3rd in the Pacific division and 12th in the Western.

Unsatisfied with the Warriors record this season, Joe Lacob made the bold decision to hire a new head coach. He ended up hiring broadcaster Mark Jackson who had no direct experience on the sideline. Many people criticized his decision and felt like he acted out of impulse. With constant changes happening around the organization Curry experienced problems with his right ankle during the off-season. Due to multiple injuries to his ankle caused in the previous season, Curry had sustained damage to his right ankle that would require surgery. In the beginning month of May in 2011, Steph underwent successful surgery to repair the damage in his right ankle. The surgery repaired instability that existed in his ankle that was caused by multiple sprains throughout the previous season. Things were looking good and doctors expected Curry to be fully ready to return for training camp in the fall. It was no question that Steph was helping the team improve their overall style of play. But next season would prove to be one of the toughest battles of Steph's career and also the whole

Warriors organization.

Chapter 7: 2011-2012 Season

(The Struggle)

After a solid season the previous year, Curry and the Warriors were determined to make the playoffs this season. Unfortunately, they would not be able to begin their fight for making playoffs as quickly as they hoped due to the NBA lockout in the start of the 2011 season. The 2011 NBA lockout was the fourth ever lockout in the history of the NBA. The lockout officially started on July 1, 2011 and concluded on December 8th, 2011. As a result of the lockout, the season was shortened from the standard 82 regular season games to 66 games.

During a lockout, teams are not allowed to sign, trade or contract any players. Players are also prohibited from entering team facilities and having access to trainers or staff. The reason for the lockout was due to the expiration of the 2005 collective bargaining agreement. The primary issues that caused conflict between the players and the owners was how revenue was to be distributed and the structure of the salary cap and luxury tax. The owners wanted to reduce the percentage of basketball related income that players would receive from 57% to 47%. The players countered back with 53%, but the owners did not agree. Owners also wanted to create a hard salary cap and higher luxury tax with the hopes of creating a more competitive landscape between teams.

The players obviously didn't agree with this proposition. Eventually the owners and players came to an agreement and the lockout was officially over on November 26th. The new collective bargaining agreement implemented a revenue split of 51%, a flexible salary cap structure and a more rigid luxury tax. Following the implementation of the new deal, players could to return to their practice facilities and begin training on December 1st.

The lockout worked in Curry's favor because it allowed him more time to properly rehabilitate his ankle following his surgery. Prior to starting the regular season following the lockout, Curry sprained his ankle in a pre-season game. It would be the start to multiple ankle sprains that followed. The slight ankle sprain during the pre-season didn't appear too serious for Curry. In the second game of the season against the Chicago Bulls, Curry left the game early due to pain in his right ankle. On January 4th 2012, the Warriors faced The San Antonio Spurs which was their fifth game of the season. Steph would go on to sprain his right ankle once again in this game and did not return to play until January 20th. He was not only extremely frustrated, but was unsure if his ankle would be able to sustain the constant injuries.

Steph continued to play, but it was visible that he was playing cautiously and was often in pain. The coaches and staff ultimately decided that it was best for Curry to take the necessary time to heal and rehabilitate his ankle. Steph played his final game that season on March 11th against the Los Angeles Clippers. He would go on to miss the remaining 28 games of the season. His future in the NBA was beginning to look murky.

Two days following that game the Warriors ended up trading Monte Ellis, Ekpe Udoh and Kwame Brown to the Milwaukee Bucks for Andrew Bogut and Stephen Jackson. The dynamic of the newly built Warriors team was shifted yet again. The dynamic duo of Curry and Monte Ellis was no longer and Curry began to worry about his future with the Warriors. With Curry out the remainder of the season and no solid point guards to lead the team, the Warriors blew their chances of making the playoffs that season. They ended the season 23-43, with 4th place in the Pacific division and 13th in the Western conference. With Curry out and constant instability in the Warriors organization, the future was uncertain.

Fan's expressed their frustration with the trade Decision of the Warriors organization on March 19th, 2012 during a half-time ceremony to honor retired Warriors player Chris Mullin. During owner Joe Lacob's speech, fans were frantically booing and not happy that the Warriors traded their best player Monte Ellis. Many fans strongly believed that Ellis and Curry could improve the franchise over the next couple of years.

Although a tough trade decision at the time, it would mean that Curry would no longer have to compete for shots with Ellis. Once Steph returned he would be the team's main offensive leader. If he could make a successful return from his injury he could be the main star for the Warriors. Little did fans know, the trade would end up opening a spot for Klay Thompson who the Warriors drafted as the 11th overall pick in the 2011 draft. Klay was also a very sharp 3-pointer shooter and took over the small guard position once Monte Ellis was traded. He stepped up big as a rookie and averaged 12.5 points, 2.4 rebounds, and 2.0 assists per game. He averaged 44.3% from the field and 41% from the 3-point line. The question remained, would Steph be able to make a successful comeback and help lead the Warriors to a playoff appearance?

Chapter 8: 2012-2013 Season

(The Return)

Following many months of extensive rehab, Steph returned to training camp for the 2012-2013 season. Steph was extremely determined to make a strong comeback and put his ankle injury behind him. He would end up suffering a minor sprain to his ankle early in the season, but nothing serious after that. Things were finally looking good for Steph and the Warriors. The Warriors were so confident in Steph that they gave him a four-year, $44 million contract extension. Curry would go on to break the record for most three-pointers made in a single season with 272, passing Ray Allen's record of 269. He also led the league with a 45.1% three-point shooting average. Curry wasn't the only one making it rain from downtown. Klay Thompson made an impressive 211 three pointers that season with a 40.1% average. The two of them together were perhaps the greatest three-point duo in the league, which coined them the term **"The Splash Brothers".** With three-point stats like that Steph and Klay quickly became dangerous from downtown.

With Steph healthy and Klay Thompson flourishing at the small guard position, it was crucial for the Warriors to continue re-building the franchise. The Warriors continued to add new young talent to their roster. In the 2012 NBA draft, the Warriors drafted the following players below:

- Harrison Barnes as the 7th pick
- Festus Ezeli as the 30th pick
- **Draymond Green as the 35th pick**
- Ognjen Kuzmic as the 52nd pick

On February 27th, 2013 Steph would go on the have a career

high 54 points against the New York Knicks, shooting 11 of 13 from the 3-point line. It was a defining moment for Curry which established him as one of the premier guards in the league. Even though the Warriors ended up losing the game 109-105, it showed fans a glimpse into what kind of superstar player Steph was becoming. He was not only evolving as a player, but he was changing the very core of the Warriors franchise. At the end of the regular season Steph averaged 22.9 points, 4.0 rebounds, and 6.9 assists per game. Despite Brandon Rush having a season-ending injury, rookie Harrison Barnes stepped up for the Warriors and was a crucial factor into helping them make the playoffs that season. The Warriors finished the 2012-2013 season with a 47- 35 record, 2nd in the Pacific division and 6th in the Western conference. Steph had helped push the Warriors to their first playoff appearance in the past 6 years. It was now time for him to continue to elevate his game and experience the intensity of the playoffs.

In their first round of the playoffs the Warriors faced the Denver Nuggets. The Warriors lost their first playoff game against the Nuggets 95-97. Curry had 19 points, but his performance wasn't enough to get the Warriors the win. The second game against the Nuggets Steph dropped 30 points along with 13 assists to help the Warriors win the game 131-117. The Warriors were confident they could win the series since the next two games were at home. In Game 3 Steph had another double-double consisting of 29 points and 11 assists. The Warriors managed to squeeze by a 110-108 win over the Nuggets. In Game 4 Steph continued to dominate. He scored 31 points, sunk 6 out of 11 threes and led the team to a 115-101 win over the Nuggets. The Warriors were now just one game away from advancing to the next round of playoffs. The Nuggets, however, were not ready to give up without a fight.

In Game 5 Curry had a bad shooting night and only managed to score 15 points. As a result of his poor performance, the Nuggets beat the Warriors 107-100. With Game 6 being a home game, Curry knew the Warriors had the advantage and was ready to lead his team to victory. Curry ended Game 6 with 22 points, 8 assists and 4 rebounds on a perfect 6-of-6 from the 3-point line. His flawless 3-point shooting performance helped the Warriors beat the Nuggets 92-88 and advance to the next round of playoffs. Fans were stunned at the kind of numbers Steph was putting up being that it was his first time in the playoffs. They were witnessing a superstar in the making.

In their second round of playoffs the Warriors faced the San Antonio Spurs, who were a very experienced team in the playoffs. The first two games were away games for the Warriors and they would have to play extremely hard if they hoped to win against the Spurs. Game 1 was a grueling double overtime battle and the Spurs managed to beat the Warriors 129-127. Steph had an incredible game scoring 44 points and racking up 11 assists. Klay also played well contributing 19 points. The Splash Brothers would have to really turn up their shooting if they stood any chance of beating the Spurs. In Game 2 the Warriors managed to beat the Spurs 100-91 led by a 34-point performance by Klay Thompson. Steph dropped 22 points and was ready to take over the next two games at home. Unfortunately, the tough Spurs defense held Steph to only 16 points and the Spurs beat the Warriors 102-92. Steph was experiencing the type of team the Warriors would need to beat in order to one day become NBA champs. Game 4 ended up going to overtime and it was another grueling game. The Warriors managed to win the game 97-87 in overtime led by a 26-point performance by Harrison Barnes and a 22-point performance by Curry. The series was now tied 2-2 and both teams were going to fight for the win.

The next two games the Spurs playoff experience showed as they crushed the Warriors in a 109-91 victory in Game 5 and a 94-82 win in Game 6. The Spurs disciplined defense wore down Steph and Klay and caused them to force bad shots inside the perimeter. The Spurs managed to hold Klay to only 4 points and Steph to only 9 points in Game 5. The Spurs ended beating the Warriors 4-2 in the series and advanced to the next round of playoffs to face the Memphis Grizzlies. It was obvious to fans and critics that the Warriors, although young and inexperienced in the playoffs, could have beaten the Spurs. During his first 12 playoff games Steph averaged 23.4 points, 8 assists and 3.8 rebounds per game. He was improving tremendously as player and a leader of the Warriors team. Warriors fans were excited to see what next season would bring and the kind of impact the Splash Brothers would have on the

league.

Chapter 9:

2013-2014 Season (Kerr)

In the 2013-2014 season the Warriors organization would end up going through a few more changes that ultimately ended up solidifying and molding the team into a powerhouse. The Splash Brothers started their season opening game strong against the Los Angeles Lakers by beating them 125-94. Steph and Klay were shooting the lights out with both shooting over 40% from the three-point line. Things were looking good for the Steph and the Warriors this season and it looked like they would have no trouble making the playoffs.

The Warriors ended up finishing the season with a 51-31 record, 2nd in the Pacific division and 6th in the Western conference. Although a slight improvement from their record the previous year of 47-35, owners Joe Lacob and Peter Guber still weren't 100% satisfied with Mark Jackson's efforts. The Warriors would end up making the playoffs again this season. Steph went on to have his best season yet averaging 24 points, 4.3 rebounds and 8.5 assists per game. Steph would also go on to have his first NBA All-Star appearance this year. He also led the league again in three-point field goals made with 261. He was excited to get the playoffs going and see how far the Warriors could go this year.

In their first round of playoffs the Warriors faced the Los Angeles Clippers. The Clippers were a solid team and point guard Chris Paul would prove to be a tough match up for Steph. Although the Warriors ended up beating the

Clippers in the first game 109-105, they held Curry to only 14 points and forced him commit 7 turnovers. Curry would have to play much smarter if he wanted to stand a good chance of winning the first round of playoffs. The next game would prove how much discipline the Warriors lacked on the defensive end. The Clippers ended up blowing them out 138-98. The Clippers forced the Warriors to a total of 26 turnovers while they only had 13. The Warriors got sloppy with the ball and got absolutely embarrassed. Their next game against the Clippers at home was much better, but Blake Griffin dominated them in the paint dropping 32 points. As a result the Warriors lost 96-98. Steph played a solid game with 16 points and 15 assists, but it wasn't enough to help the Warriors get the win. They were now down 2-1 in the series and would have to make a serious defensive adjustment if they hoped to win the next game.

In Game 4 the Splash Brother came to play combing for a total of 48 points, 33 points from Curry and 15 points from Klay. The Warriors ended up winning the game and it was thanks to Steph's incredible shooting. The series were now tied 2-2 and it was back to Los Angeles for Game 5.

Game 5 proved to be very difficult for Steph as the Clippers defense bullied him around and forced to commit a total of 8 turnovers. DeAndre Jordan from the Clippers was an absolute bully in the paint snatching 18 rebounds and scoring 25 points. The Clippers strong defense helped them win the game 113-103. Steph was seriously disappointed with how careless he was with the ball and knew it was a huge determining factor to their loss. He would have to be a more careful passer if he wanted the Warriors to stand a chance in Game 6. It was back to the Oracle Arena for Game 6 and the Warriors were a very hard team to beat at home. Steph hoped that the energy of the crowd would help push his team to play more aggressively.

Game 6 turned out to be another nail bitter of a game. Curry led his team with 24 points, 4 rebounds and 9 assists. Every quarter in Game 6 had less than a 7-point advantage from each team and the Warriors managed to squeeze out a 100-99 victory late in the 4th quarter. It was no doubt that Game 7 was going to be an all-out war. Curry would have to play at his best if he had hopes of helping his team advance to the next round of playoffs. It was back to the Staples

lead the Warriors to a 67-15 regular season record. His performance this season put him in the top running for MVP candidate along with James Harden, LeBron James and Russell Westbrook. In the end Steph would end up being the 2014-2015 NBA season MVP. It was an achievement he had always dreamed of when he was a kid and his relentless work ethic and dedication to the game helped him achieve his goal.

He owed much of his success this season to coach Kerr. Curry realized the importance of coach Kerr's system given the young talent and skillset of the Warriors team. Coach Kerr stressed the importance of proper ball movement and spacing to get the best possible shots for the team given Steph and Klay's high shooting percentage behind the arc. Coach Kerr connected well with all the Warriors players and made some changes in the lineup that rubbed many critics and analysts the wrong way. His coaching style was a bit unorthodox, but it transformed the Warriors into a lethal team. Coach Kerr utilized the players so well and created a team chemistry that was unrivaled. Numerous Warriors players set their own individual records throughout the season.

Apart from Curry's MVP award and his three-point record, Klay Thompson went on to have his best season yet. In the 2014-2015 season Klay averaged 21.7 points, 3.2 rebounds, and 2.9 assists per game. On January 23rd, 2015 Klay broke the NBA record for most point scored in a single quarter with 37. That same game he also went on to have a career high of 52 points. That same season Curry and Thompson broke the single-season record for most three-pointers made by a pair of teammates with 525 three-pointers. It was more than obvious that the addition of coach Kerr made a massive difference in the Warriors franchise. The Warriors finished the season with a 67-15 record and finished 1st in the Pacific division and 1st in the Western conference. The real question stood, would to Warriors break under playoff pressure again? Would Curry be able to lift the Warriors and lead them to the promise land?

In their first round of playoffs the Warriors faced off against the New Orleans Pelicans. There was much speculation about how Curry and the Warriors would perform in the playoffs since it was Steve Kerr's first time in the playoffs as a coach. Would he be able to handle the intensity and pressure of the playoffs? It was no doubt that the Warriors were a different team with coach Kerr by their side. The Warriors ended up sweeping the New Orleans Pelicans in four games and made their first round of playoffs look effortless. They were playing in sync, limiting their turnovers and shooting extremely well behind the arc. They closed the gap in their lack of consistency during the playoffs and it was apparent to fans and critics that the Warriors would be very difficult to beat.

In their second round of playoffs the Warriors faced the Memphis Grizzlies. Things were off to a hot start with the Warriors beating the Grizzlies by 15 points in the first game. Steph and Klay combined for 40 points in the first game and their victory looked easy. The next few games the Grizzlies would prove to be a challenge. Game 2 of the second round of playoffs was extremely close every quarter, but the Grizzlies would end up winning the game 97-90. Steph's three-point shooting was terrible in Game 2, making only 2 out of 11. Steph finished the game with only 19 points and it was obvious that the Grizzlies forced him to take high pressured three's when he should have moved the ball around more.

Game 3 would end up being very similar to Game 2 with the Grizzlies stealing yet another win over the Warriors with a final score of 99-89. Steph continued to struggle from the three-point line in Game 3 making only 2 out of 10 threes. Coach Kerr knew that the team needed to shift their game around if they hoped to stay in the playoffs. Things were beginning to look bad for the Warriors. They needed to move the ball around more and stop taking forced shots and that's exactly what they ended up doing in Game 4. Steph buckled down and started leading his team. The Warriors ended up blowing out the Grizzlies 101-84 in Game 4 and knew exactly how they needed to play in order to win the remaining games. Steph would finish Game 4 with 33 points on an 11 out of 22 from the field.

The next two games the Warriors continued to move the ball around and capitalized on smarter shots from inside the perimeter. They ended up beating the Grizzlies in the second round of playoffs and advanced to the next round. It became apparent that Steph was molding into a leader that could take the Warriors to the finals and with Steve Kerr and the helm, they were ready change the very core of the Warriors franchise.

In the next round and playing for the Western Conference finals championship, the Warriors faced the Houston Rockets. The Rockets were a stacked team with superstar James Harden leading the way. Game 1 was an extremely close game with plenty of lead changes and neither team leading by more than 7 points during the whole course of the game. The Warriors ended up beating the Rockets 110-106 and it was obvious they would be a tough team to beat going forward. Steph finished the game with 34 points on a 6 of 11 from the three-point line. He was taking smarter shots and helping the rest of his teammates perform to the best of their abilities.

Game 2 would also prove to be a very close game which the Warriors also ended up winning by just a single point. The final score of Game 2 was 99-98. Steph dropped 33 points along with 6 assists to lead the Warriors to victory. James Harden played an incredible game dropping 38 points along with 9 assists. With Games 3 and 4 being away games, Steph and the Warriors needed to make sure to not let the pressure get to them. In Game 3 the Warriors would go on to absolutely blow out the Rockets by 35 points and they were now one game away from advancing to the NBA finals. Fans could see the kind of player Steph was evolving to and how big of an impact he was having on the rest of his teammates. Steph finished Game 3 with 40 points, 7 assists and 5 rebounds. He made 7 out of 9 three-pointers and helped the rest of his teammates take smart shots in order to seal a Game 3 victory over the Rockets.

In Game 4 the Warriors got sloppy with the ball and committed 29 personal fouls which would cause them to lose Game 4 with a final score of 115-128. Steph knew that as the leading point guard of the team he needed to make sure his teammates didn't cave under pressure. He was determined to get to the finals and win Game 5. With Game 5 being back home at the Oracle Arena, Steph wanted to win the game for the home crowd and prove to them that he was ready to bring a championship to the Warriors franchise.

Although the Rockets forced the Warriors to 30 personal fouls in Game 5 the Warriors managed to win the game 104-90. Steph finished the game with 26 points, 8 rebounds and 6 assists. Even though Steph had a rough night of shooting from behind arc, sinking only 3 out 11 three-pointers, the rest of his teammates played extremely well on the offensive end. Klay Thompson finished the night with 20 points and Harrison Barnes came up big with 24 points to help push the team to victory and advance to the NBA finals. Steph had accomplished a goal that many players only dream of. After only 6 years in the league, Steph not only evolved as a player and a leader, but he led his team to the NBA finals.

The Warriors faced off against the Cleveland Cavaliers in the 2015 NBA finals. Steph would have to play against one of the best players in the league, LeBron James. Not only did the Cavaliers have LeBron James, but they also had one of the best point guards in the league, Kyrie Irving. They were a dynamic duo that played extremely well with each other and Steph would have to seriously step up his leadership if he hoped to push his team to victory. Game 1 was on June 4th at the Oracle Arena and the Warriors were very tough to beat at home. Steph would seriously have to focus on helping his teammates limit the number of turnovers because the Cavaliers would capitalize on them with LeBron and Kyrie being so strong on the offensive end. Steph helped the Warriors do just that. They played smart and only committed 16 turnovers in the game and moved the ball around quickly in order to take open shots. The Warriors ended up winning Game 1 with a final score of 108-100. It was certainly a close game and it was obvious LeBron wanted to win just as badly as Steph. LeBron finished the game with 44 points, 8 rebounds and 6 assists while Steph dropped 26 points, 4 rebounds and 8 assists. It was apparent to everyone that the Cavaliers would make Steph and the Warriors work hard for every point they scored.

Game 2 would end up being another extremely close game, but the Cavs would end up snatching a 95-93 victory over the Warriors. The Cavs were all over Steph and forced him to take terrible shots which led to him having a terrible shooting night making only 2 of 15 threes. This was perhaps one of Steph's worst shooting performance of his career. LeBron on the other hand, dominated in Game 2 and had a triple double consisting of 39 points, 16 rebounds and 11 assists. It quickly became obvious to Steph that if the Warriors wanted to win, they would have to figure out a way to slow down LeBron. Games 3 and 4 were back at the Quicken Loans Arena, in Cleveland Ohio. The Cav's were extremely strong playing at home and Steph would have to elevate his game to the next level if he hoped to win the finals.

Game 3 would end being a very close game with tons of lead changes that made Cleveland's arena rumble with excitement anytime LeBron or Kyrie scored a basket. Although the game was extremely close, the Cavs went on a small scoring spree in the 4th quarter and won Game 3 with a final score of 96-91. Even though the Cavs won, Steph had an amazing performance consisting of 27 points, 6 rebounds and 6 assists. The Warriors were heading into dangerous territory by losing Game 3. They were now down 2-1 in the finals and if the Cav's end up winning Game 4, Steph knew that their chances of winning the title would be far out of reach. No NBA team has ever come back from 3-1 deficit in the finals to win the title. In Game 4 the Warriors turned things around and beat the Cavs 103-82 and tied the series 2-2. With Kyrie Irving being out for the remainder of the finals due to a fractured kneecap late in Game 3, the Warriors held a huge advantage over the Cavs.

Even though it appeared that the Warriors had an advantage over the Cavaliers, Steph knew the kind of superstar player that LeBron was. They couldn't get comfortable. The Warriors ended up taking advantage of the fact that Kyrie was out for the remainder of the finals and won Game 5 with a 104-91 victory over the Cavs. Steph had an incredible game consisting of 37 points, 7 rebounds and 4 assists. He lifted his team to the next level and the Warriors were only one game away from being NBA champions. Although they won the game, they still failed to slow down LeBron as he dropped yet another massive triple double consisting of 40 points, 14 rebounds and 11 assists. Game 6 was back at the Quicken Loans Arena and Steph was determined to win the game and bring home a championship to Golden State.

Steph and the Warriors took an early 13-point lead in the first quarter and the game quickly shifted in their favor.

Some sloppy ball handling and poor shot selection by the Warriors in the second quarter helped the Cavaliers close the 13-point gap and at the end of the second quarter the Warriors only led the game 45-43. It was obvious that LeBron was not going to let the championship slip by. At the start of the third quarter the Warriors quickly pulled the lead away and the Cavaliers would fail to ever make a comeback.

The final score of the game was 105-97. The Warriors had done it. They had become the 2015 NBA champions. In just his sixth season in the NBA, Steph had brought home a championship to the Golden State franchise and solidified himself as one of the best players in the league. Steph finished the game with 25 points, 6 rebounds and 8 assists. His teammate Andre Iquodala received the 2015 NBA finals MVP award and it was heavily argued that the award should have gone to Steph. Nonetheless, Steph was proud of how much his team improved and how hard they played together in order to win the championship. After a long and successful season, the Warriors took some much-needed time off to rest and get mentally and physically ready for the next season. Would they be able to win another championship the following season?

Chapter 11: 2015-2016 Season

(The Streak)

After an extremely successful season, winning the league MVP award and leading his team to a NBA championship, Steph continued to work on his game and his relationship with his teammates and coach Steve Kerr. During the offseason the team's bond and chemistry improved and the Warriors were ready to make another run at the NBA title. The 2015-16 season would end up being another record-breaking season for not only Steph, but the Warriors franchise as well. The regular season flew by and the Warriors broke record after record, all under the leadership of their star point guard Steph Curry.

To begin his 2015-2016 season, Steph became the first player since Michael Jordan in his 1989-90 season to score 118 points in his team's first three games of the regular season. He scored 40 points in the first game of the season, 25 games in the second and a whopping 53 points in the third game. Not only was he having an incredible start to his season, but the Warriors made history on November 24th when they became the first team to start a season with a record of 16-0. They continued their impressive streak to 24-0 on December 11th with a win over the Boston Celtics. Their streak was finally ended by the Milwaukee Bucks on December 12th.

This record shattering start to their season made the Warriors a feared team and Steph gained recognition as the greatest shooter in NBA history. During the 2016 NBA All-Star Weekend, Steph made his third straight NBA All-Star appearance for the West and competed in the Three-Point Shootout challenge against his own teammate Klay Thompson. At the end of their regular season the Warriors surpassed the 1995-1996 Chicago Bulls' 72-10 record to finish the season at 73-9. It was truly an incredible record breaking season not only for Steph, but for the Warriors franchise as a whole.

At the end of the 2015-2016 season Steph had made 402 three-pointers, no other player (himself included) had ever made more than 300 threes in a single NBA season. The only other player to come close to him that season in three's made with 276 was his own teammate Klay Thompson. Steph averaged 30.1 points, 5.4 rebounds, 6.7 assists and 2.1 steals per game. Steph also once again led the league in free-throw percentage in the 2015-2016 season with 90.80% .These kinds of performances weren't a fluke, Steph is simply that gifted of a shooter. For that reason Steph became the first player to be named the league's first ever unanimous MVP, becoming only the 11th player in NBA history to win the prestigious award in two consecutive seasons. Steph had carved his name in the record books and established himself as a global superstar in the sport of basketball. All eyes and critics quickly shifted to how the Steph and the Warriors would perform in the playoffs and there was much speculation that they would easily win another NBA title this year.

In their first round of playoffs the Warriors faced the Houston Rockets. Up until now, Steph had almost forgotten about his troublesome ankle that had bothered him in the past and almost sent his career in the gutter. In Game 1 against the Rockets Steph tweaked his ankle getting back on defense in just the first half of the game. Fans and critics alike quickly began to speculate on the severity of his injury and how his absence put the Warriors hopes of chasing a second title in jeopardy. Steph would go on to miss Games 2, 3 and 5 against the Rockets, but the Warriors still ended up beating the Rockets in 5 games without much trouble. The only game the Houston Rockets managed to win against the Warriors was Game 3 by a single point. The Warriors were so good that they ended up beating the Rockets by an average of twenty-four points in the other four games.

Their next opponent in the second round was the

Portland Trail Blazers. Still dealing with his ankle injury, Steph ended up sitting out the first three games against the Trail Blazers. Luckily for Steph and the Warriors, Klay Thompson stepped up huge in his absence and dropped 37 points in Game 1, 27 points Game 2 and 35 points in Game 3 to put the Warriors up 2-1 against Portland. Once Steph made his return in Game 4 he dropped 40 points and helped the Warriors secure a 132-125 win over the Trail Blazers and then 29 points in Game 5 to help them advance to the next round of playoffs. Despite Steph's troublesome injuries early on in the playoffs, the Warriors still managed to beat teams without much trouble. Their next opponent, the Oklahoma City Thunder would prove to be their toughest matchup so far. It would be the series that would later go on to create some of the biggest superstars in the NBA today. No one could have predicted the impact the outcome of this series would go on to have in the NBA.

The Oklahoma City Thunder was absolutely stacked with superstar talent. They had arguably one of the best players in the NBA Kevin Durant, alongside one of the best point guards in the league Russell Westbrook. The two together were a lethal combination unlike anything the league had ever seen before. To top it off, they had Serge Ibaka and Steven Adams who had dominating size and power over the Warriors roster. With Game 1 being a home game at the Oracle Arena, Steph and the Warriors hoped to get a quick win to establish early dominance in the series. Although it would end up being an extremely close game, Kevin Durant and Russell Westbrook ended up out-playing the Splash brothers in an incredible second-half comeback. Despite the home loss, Steph still managed to put up 26 point sand scoop up 10 rebounds against guys that were almost a foot taller than him. In Game 2 the Warriors held Russell Westbrook to only 16 points and had a very strong defensive game along with a strong performance from their bench players which helped them seal a 118-91 victory over the Thunder. Steph Curry dropped 28 points and shot over 60% from the field to help get the Warriors the win.

With Games 3 and 4 being away games at the Chesapeake Energy Arena in Oklahoma, Steph and the Warriors had to play at their absolute best or their chances of winning a title could slip away. In Game 3 Russell

Westbrook and Kevin Durant caught fire and combined for 63 points and ended up dismantling the Warriors in a 133-105 blowout victory. It became evident to Steph that he would have to play a different type of game when facing strong opponents on their home court. It was a type of competition that the Warriors were not properly ready for.

As a result of their lack of preparation, the Warriors also ended up losing Game 4 with a final score of 118-94. The Warriors were now down 3-1 in the series against the Thunder and it would take a miracle for them to come back and win. They would have to win 3 straight games in order beat the Thunder. Game 5 was back at the Oracle Arena for the Warriors and Steph was ready to turn things up for the fans at home. It would be an extremely close game quarter by quarter, but the Warriors managed to win the game 120-111. Steph and Klay Thompson would go on to combine for 58 points along with plenty of help from their bench players in order to get the win. It was a team effort that helped them get the win and remain in the playoffs. Game 6 was back at the Chesapeake Energy Arena in Oklahoma City. Having gotten blown out by more than twenty points in Games 3 and 4, Steph was ready to play carefully in Game 6 and take smarter shots behind the arc. Despite a very close game the Warriors managed to play better and won the game 96-88. Steph had an incredible game consisting of 31 points, 10 rebounds and 9 assists, just one assist shy of a triple double. He made 7 out of 12 three-pointers and took smart shots that showed his ability to adjust his game in tough situations. The series was now tied 3-3 and fans and critics couldn't wait to see how Game 7 would unfold. It was certain that Game 7 would be an all-out war.

With Game 7 being back home at the Oracle Arena, the Warriors held a slight advantage over the Thunder. Steph knew that this game would be his defining moment as a player and a leader of his team. This game was one that he did not want to lose. There was simply too much on the line.

Right after tipoff both teams looked paranoid and ready to put it all on the line. The sold-out crowd at the Oracle Arena made the game much more intense. With every shot the Warriors sunk the fans were on their feet and cheering. At the end of the first half of the game the Thunder led the Warriors 48 to 42. Steph knew his team was down

every possession until someone scored. Many players can get the crowd loud and off their feet, but only a few players can silence them.

By the end of the third quarter the score was 76-75 with the Warriors in the lead by just one point. One thing was for certain, the 4th quarter would go down in history as one of the most memorable of Steph's career. With the start of the 4th quarter LeBron James made a 5-foot jumper that put the Cavaliers up by one point. The rest of the 4th quarter stayed extremely close. In the closing minutes of the 4th quarter Andre Iquadola was on a fast break and LeBron James would deliver what would become known as **"The Block".** With the score tied at 89-89 with 1:50 remaining in the game J.R Smith from the Cavaliers would end up getting the defensive rebound following LeBron's block and Kyrie Irving shot and made a 25-foot three pointer to put the Cavs up 92-89. The Warriors would fail to score again and the Cleveland Cavaliers became the 2016 NBA champs. It was a series that Steph and the Warriors would never forget. Steph had played his heart out during this season and established himself as one of the best players and shooters in the league. The Cavaliers became the first team in NBA history to come back from a 3-1 deficit in the finals and win. Steph held his head high after the game and was determined to become a better player in the offseason and get ready to make another run at the Cavaliers next season. One thing was for certain, Steph was not finished, he was just getting started.

Chapter 12: 2016-2017 Season

(Round 3)

Following a record-breaking regular season in 2015-2016, Steph and the Warriors were determined to make another run for the NBA title. The championship literally slipped through their fingertips and they were itching for a chance to redeem themselves. During the off-season the Warriors made a power move and acquired free agent Kevin Durant and were quickly hailed as a **"Superteam"** by fans, critics and major media outlets. They became the fierce four consisting of Kevin Durant, Stephen Curry, Klay Thompson and Draymond Green. This kind of superstar lineup could elevate Steph's game to another level and make the Warriors into one of the most powerful teams in NBA history. With Kevin Durant on their roster, making the playoffs was inevitable.

Steph continued to shoot the lights out in the 2016-2017 season making 324 threes with a 41.1% shooting average behind the arc. Although this would be his lowest shooting percentage yet, it still left him second all-time in the history books, chasing only his own records. Steph went on to average 25.3 points, 4.5 rebounds and 6.6 assists in the 2016-2017 season. On November 7th, Steph broke the record for the most three-pointers made in a single game with 13, beating his previous record of 12 held jointly by himself, Kobe Bryant and Donyell Marshall. Looking at Steph's shooting, we can see that it was impacted by the addition of Kevin Durant, but not necessarily in a negative way. As a result of adding Kevin Durant, Steph ended up taking four less field goal attempts per 36 minutes which isn't a big deal considering the kind of contribution Kevin Durant made in his first season with the Warriors. In his first season with the

Warriors, Kevin Durant averaged 25.1 points, 8.3 rebounds and 4.8 assists per game. His addition to the Warriors helped take off a decent amount of pressure from Steph and truly molded the Warriors into a **"Superteam"**.

The Warriors shattered over 20 NBA records in the 2016-2017 season and finished with regular season record of 67-15 which tied their 2014-2015 regular season record. At the end of the regular season, the Warriors secured the top seed in the playoffs for the third consecutive year. Their performance in the playoffs was nothing like fans or critics had seen before. They were demolishing teams with ease.

In their first round of playoffs they faced the Portland Trail Blazers. They ended up sweeping them in four games And winning each game by an average of 18 points. In those four games against the Trail Blazers Steph averaged over 29 points per game and shot over 40% from the field. They would also end up sweeping the Utah Jazz in their second round of playoffs and also the San Antonio Spurs. Steph and the Warriors were now back to the NBA finals for the third consecutive year facing LeBron James and the Cleveland Cavaliers. Up until this point the Warriors had not lost any playoffs games. If there was one team that could stop their streak, it was the Cavaliers. Having suffered an unprecedented loss in the finals to the Cavaliers the previous season, Steph knew how the Warriors needed to play in order to take home the NBA title.

In Game 1 of the 2017 NBA finals Steph and the Warriors were determined to make a statement against the Cavaliers in front of their fans at the Oracle Arena. The Warriors ended up blowing out the Cavaliers 113-91 and it shocked fans how easily the Warriors managed to win against arguably the best player in the world, LeBron James. Regardless of how good LeBron was, Steph had transformed as a player and a leader. In Game 2 against the Cavaliers, Steph led his team to a 132-113 victory by racking up a triple double consisting of 32 points, 10 rebounds and 11 assists. Kevin Durant dropped 33 points and 13 rebounds and Klay Thompson scored 22 points along with 7 rebounds to help the Warriors get the win. The Warriors were now up 2-0 in the finals and showed no signs of breaking their playoff streak. With the next two games being away at the Quicken Loans Arena in Cleveland Ohio,

Steph was determined to sweep the Cavaliers in front of their home crowd. Many people believed that the Cavaliers comeback win in the finals was a fluke and Steph wanted to prove so by sweeping them in four games and beating them at home. It was obvious that LeBron was determined to not let that happen.

In Game 3 LeBron dropped 39 points, 11 rebounds and 9 assists, just 1 assist shy of a triple double. Kyrie Irving dropped 38 points along with 6 rebounds. Although LeBron and Kyrie had incredible performances and the game was extremely close, Steph and the Warriors managed to win the game 118-113. With the Game 3 win over the Cavaliers the Warriors became the first team in all professional sports to start 15-0 in the postseason. The Warriors were just one game away from wining the NBA title and having a perfect 16-0 postseason record. Unfortunately, the Cavaliers would go on to stop them in their pursuit of a perfect postseason record. The Cavaliers ended up beating the Warriors 137-116 and managed to escape an embarrassing four game sweep at home.

Game 5 was back at the Oracle Arena and Steph was

excited to bring home a championship in front of his home fans. This time the Warriors were not going to allow the Cavaliers to have a comeback. Steph would go onto have a 34-point performance while Kevin Durant poured in 39 points to help the Warriors secure a 129-120 victory over the Cavaliers. The Warriors had done it again. They were the 2017 NBA champions. They also went on to set the best playoff record in NBA history by going 16-1. Kevin Durant was crowned the 2017 NBA Finals MVP. Steph now had two rings and there was nothing stopping him in his pursuit of continuing to win and improve as a leader and a player. It was truly an incredible season filled with many record-breaking moments individually and as a team. In the 2016-2017 season the Warriors broke over 20 NBA records. Below is a list of the individual, team and franchise records broken in the 2016-2017 season.

INDIVIDUAL

- Most three-pointers made in a single game -**13** (Stephen Curry)

- Most consecutive regular-season games with twenty or more points- **72** (Kevin Durant)
- Most consecutive games (regular season + postseason combined) with a three-pointer made - **196** (Stephen Curry)
- Most consecutive regular-season games with a made three-pointer -**157** (Stephen Curry)
- Most consecutive regular-season games with a made three-pointer on the road - **117** (Stephen Curry)
- Most consecutive playoff games with a made three-pointer -**75** (Stephen Curry)
- First player to score 60 points in a game in under 30 minutes (Klay Thompson against the Indiana Pacers on December 5, 2016)
- First player to record a triple-double while scoring fewer than 10 points (Draymond Green, 12 rebounds, 10 assists, 10 steals)
- Most three-pointers made in a four-game playoff series – 21 (Stephen Curry)

TEAM

- Best start in the postseason (15 – 0)
- Best record in the NBA postseason (16 -1)
- Longest winning streak in a postseason (15 games)

- Most games without back-to-back losses in a regular-season – **146** (April 9th, 2015 – March 2nd, 2017)
- First team to have four players hit **four three-pointers** in a single game – Durant, Curry, Klay, Draymond green
- Most combined three-point attempts in a single game – **88** (Warriors and Houston Rockets shot 44 three-pointers on December 1st 2016)
- Most games with a 40-point winning margin or higher in a regular-season- **3** (tied five other teams for the NBA record)
- Most players in the All-Star Game – **4** (Durant, Curry, Klay, Draymond)
- Most points in a playoff game, first quarter – **45** points (shared with 3 other teams)
- Playoff point-differential per game entering NBA Finals **+16.3**
- Fewest turnovers in a NBA Finals game - **4** (Game 1, tied with 2 other teams)
- Most three-pointers in an NBA Finals quarter – **9** (Game 3)
- Most three-pointers in an NBA finals half – **12** (Game 3)

FRANCHISE RECORDS

- Most steals in a single game – **10** (Draymond Green, NBA record is 11)
- Most consecutive games with a made three-pointer at home – **107** (Stephen Curry, NBA record is 132 by Kyle Korver)
- Only Warriors player to score 60 points or more in a game – Klay Thompson
- Point-differential per game in a regular-season **+ 11.63** (fourth highest in NBA history)
- Most games with 30 or more assists in a regular-season – **50**
- Most assists in a game – **47**
- Most assists per game in a regular-season – **30.4** (fifth highest in NBA history)
- Most assists in a regular-season – **2,491** (fifth most in NBA history)
- Most games in a row with 30+ assists – **10**
- Most games in a season with 40 + assists – **3**
- Most three-pointers attempted in a game – **48**
- Fewest turnovers in a playoff game – **7**
- Most assists in a half in the postseason – **23**
- Playoff point-differential per game – **13.5** (second biggest winning margin in NBA history)

Chapter 13: 2017-2018 Season

(Round 4)

After a record-breaking season and winning the 2017 NBA title, Steph and the Warriors had no plans of slowing down. They wanted to continue dominating the NBA and rack up as many titles as they could. The Warriors organization was so confident in Steph that on July 1st, 2017 they inked him the first ever 200-million-dollar contract to a five-year maximum with no options. The contract would go on to carry Steph through the 2021-22 season carving a foundational piece for the future of the Warrior's potential dynasty.

Many other teams in the NBA saw the Warriors as the main team to beat. As a result of the Warriors going to the finals for three straight seasons in a row, many NBA teams began to restructure their roster. The Houston Rockets ended up acquiring star point guard Chris Paul from the Los Angelus Clippers to play alongside James Harden. The Oklahoma City Thunder acquired Paul George from the Indiana Pacers to play alongside superstar Russell Westbrook. The Cavs added George Hill and Rodney Hood to try and address their two biggest needs: their defense and poor guard play. The Detroit Pistons made some huge moves in their roster for Blake Griffin with the Clippers. All NBA teams were making huge restructuring moves in order to try and compete with the Warriors. The Warriors were a direct result of the kind of player Stephen Curry became and also because of coach Kerr's unique coaching style. The Warriors roster was also very young which put them at a significant advantage over other teams. They could play for another half a decade and dominate with ease.

Steph was excited to get the new season started and continue improving his game so the Warriors could make another run at the championship this year. Little did he know, this season would prove to be one of the most difficult of his career. Ankle injuries threatened Steph's career early on, but he was able to recover and lead the Warriors to two championships. This season Steph would go on to suffer a long list of random injuries that would cause him to miss 31 regular season games along with 6 playoff games. The injuries frustrated Steph and made him think about his long-term future in the league. Below is a timeline of the injuries Steph suffered in the 2017-2018 season and how many games he missed as a result.

- **November 12th, 2017** – Right thigh contusion – 1 game missed
- **November 26th, 2017** – Right hand contusion – 1 game missed
- **December 4th , 2017** – Sprained right ankle – 11 games missed

- **January 10th, 2018** – Sprained right ankle – 2 games missed
- **March 2nd, 2018** – Sprained right ankle – no games missed
- **March 8th, 2018** – Sprained right ankle – 6 games missed
- **March 23rd, 2018** – Sprained left MCL – 10 regular season games and 6 playoff games

It's obvious to see that Steph's major underlying injury and threat to his career is his right ankle. Even though Steph missed that many games the Warriors still managed to finish the season with a record of 58-24. Their record put them 1st in the Pacific division, and 2nd in the Western conference behind the Houston Rockets. Even though Steph missed plenty of games this season, he still made a huge impact on his team. He averaged 26.4 points, 5.1 rebounds and 6.1 assists per game.

Heading into the playoffs many fans and analysts had doubts that the Warriors would be able to get past the Spurs in the first round since Steph was still out due to his injury. Even with Steph out for the first round of playoffs, the Warriors beat the Spurs without much trouble in just five games. It was obvious the Warriors were a hard team to beat even without Steph leading the way. Steph would return in the second game of the second round of playoffs against the New Orleans Pelicans. In his first game back against the Pelicans Steph dropped 28 points, 7 rebounds and 2 assists to help the Warriors win the game 121-116. He also ended up shooting 50% from the three-point line. Fans were happy to have him back and leading the Warriors in the playoffs. The Warriors ended up beating the Pelicans in just five games and were ready to continue their quest for another title.

Their next opponent, the Houston Rockets, would prove to be the most challenging so far. In Game 1, Steph had a quite game of only 18 points due to the tight defensive pressure that was deployed on him by the Rockets. They knew he was their go to shooter and planned to do everything to stop him from getting hot behind the three-point line. The Warriors ended up winning Game 1 with a final score of 119-106. In Game 2 the Rockets turned up their defensive pressure on Steph holding him to only 16 points and as a result the Warriors lost 127-105. No other team in the playoffs had managed to beat the Warriors by such a large deficit and shut down Steph offensively.

With Game 3 being a home game for the Warriors, Steph was determined to win and put on a show for his home crowd. In Game 3 the Warriors proved why they were the best team in the NBA and absolutely dismantled the Houston Rockets beating them 126-85. It was one of the biggest deficits in playoffs history. Steph dropped 35 points and shot an impressive 56% from the field. Steph had figured out the way he needed to play against the high-pressure defense of the Rockets in order to win. Although an impressive win for the Warriors, the Rockets were not going down without a fight.

In Game 4 the Rockets managed to squeeze out a 95-92 victory over the Warriors and even up the series at 2-2. Steph's 28-point performance in Game 4 was simply not enough to get them the win. In Game 5 the Warriors ended up losing another tight game 98-94. They were now in troublesome territory and needed to win the next two games or they would be out of the playoffs. Game 6 was a home game for the Warriors, and they were not going to let their home crowd down. In Game 6 the Splash brother played in full force making 14 out of 28 three-pointers. It was an incredible shooting performance that helped the Warriors win the game 115-86. Steph finished the game with 29 points while Klay Thompson came up big with 35 points. With the series now tied at 3-3, it all came down to one game.

With the Houston Rockets holding home court advantage in Game 7, Steph knew he could not let his team crumble. At halftime the Houston Rockets were in the lead 54-43. Steph knew that he needed to help his team perform better in order to win the game. In the third quarter the Warriors began to get more aggressive on the defensive end and managed to score 33 points while the Rockets only scored 15 points. At the end of the third quarter the Warriors were up 76-69. At the start of the 4th quarter Klay Thompson sunk a 23-foot jumper followed by a three-pointer from Steph to put the Warriors in the lead 80-71. The Warriors continued to stay aggressive on the defensive end and forced the Rockets to take shots around the perimeter. At the 7:13 mark Steph made a deep three which put the Warriors up 89-

76. It was a lead that the Rockets would fail to come back from and the Warriors ended up winning the game 101-92. They had once again advanced to the NBA finals to face none other than LeBron James and the Cleveland Cavaliers. It became one of the biggest sports rivalries of all time.

   With Kyrie Irving being traded away to the Boston Celtics, the Cavaliers didn't have a strong point guard leading them. In Game 1 LeBron made a statement that he was not giving up on winning a championship by dropping 51 points, 8 rebounds and 8 assists. Although a star studded performance by LeBron, it would not be enough to beat the Warriors. The Warriors ended up winning the game 124-114 in front of their fans at the Oracle Arena. Steph led his team in scoring with 29 points, 6 rebounds and 9 assists. The Warriors ended up winning the next three games without any trouble and became the 2018 NBA champions. Steph had become a three-time champion and in the process helped create one of the best teams the NBA has ever seen.

Chapter 14:

Life Outside the NBA

Many fans and critics know Steph as one of the greatest shooters of all time and possibly one of the best point guards of all time, but there is more to him than meets the eye. He is a brother, father, husband and a man of faith. Every member of Steph's family has been involved in sports in one way or another. Starting with his father Dell Curry, who played in the NBA for the Charlotte Hornet's and is their all-time leader in points with (**9,839**) at the time of writing this book. Dell Curry also holds the record for three-point field goals made with (**929**) for the Charlotte Hornets'. Steph's mother Sonya Adams played volleyball and basketball at Virginia tech and has won state championship in both sports. When the topic of sibling rivalry comes up, its either about his brother Seth Curry or his sister Sydel Curry. His brother Seth Curry also plays in the NBA and his sister, like Steph's mother, is also an avid college volleyball player. Their family is very involved in sports and enjoys competition.

Apart from his siblings and parents, Steph is married to Ayesha Curry. They have three kids together named Riley, Ryan and Canon. Off the court, Steph has been involved in multiple charitable organizations to help give back to the less fortunate. Below are some of the different charities he is involved in.

- Animal Rescue Foundation
- United Nations Foundation
- Nothing But Nets Foundation

Steph also takes time in the offseason to travel all over the world fighting causes such as AIDS, animals, children, environment, health, human rights, peace, and women's rights.

On and off the court, Steph is giving back to the community and making a difference in the lives of others. If there is one thing that is certain about the two-time NBA MVP champ is that he has a strong belief in himself and in God. His faith is his foundation for his strong work ethic, leadership and commitment to not only the game of basketball but to his family and loved ones. A truly leader on and off the court.

Chapter 15:

Records

NBA RECORDS

- 3 Time NBA Champion: **2015, 2017, 2018**
- 2 Time MVP: **2015, 2016**
- 7 Time NBA All-Star: **2014, 2015, 2016, 2017, 2018, 2019**
- All-Rookie First Team: **2010**
- NBA scoring leader: **2016**
- 5 Time NBA three-point field goals leader: **2013, 2014, 2015, 2016, 2017**
- 3 Time NBA free-throw percentage leader: **2011, 2015, 2016**

- 1 Time NBA steals leader: **2016**
- NBA Three-point Contest Winner: **2015**
- NBA Skills Challenge Champion: **2011**
- NBA Sportsmanship Award: **2011**
- NBA Community Assist Award: **2014**
- NBA Regular Season record for most three-pointers made: **402**
- NBA Record for most three-pointers made in a single playoffs: **98**
- NBA Finals record for most three-pointers made in a game: **9**
- NBA record for most consecutive regular season games with a made three-pointer: **157**
- NBA record for most consecutive playoff games with a made three-pointer: **90**
- NBA record for the most 10 plus three pointer games in a regular season: **9**
- NBA record for the most points scored in an overtime period: **17**

FRANCHISE RECORDS

- Warriors franchise leader in three-point field goals made
- Warriors franchise leader in assists in playoffs
- Warriors franchise leader in three-point field goals in playoffs
- Warriors franchise leader in steals in playoffs
- Warriors franchise leader in points in playoffs
- Warriors franchise record holder for triple doubles as a rookie

COLLEGE (DAVIDSON)

- 2 Time SoCon Player of the Year (2008-2009)
- 2 Time First-Team All-SoCon (2008-2009)
- 2 Time SoCon Conference Tournament Most Outstanding Player (2007-2008)
- 3 Time SoCon first-team All-Tournament (2007 - 2008)
- SoCon Freshman of the Year (2007)
- SoCon All-Freshman Team (2007)
- Consensus first-team All-American (2009)
- Consensus second-team All-American (2008)
- NCAA Division 1 scoring leader (2009)
- Single-Season NCAA 3-point field goals (**162**, 2007-2008)
- Single-Season NCAA freshman 3-point field goals (**122**, 2006-2007)
- All-Time leading scorer in Davidson College history (**2,635**)
- All-Time Davidson College leader in 3-point field-goals made (**414**)
- All-Time Davidson college leader in 30-point games (**30**)
- Single-season Davidson college points (**974**, 2008-2009)
- Single-season Davidson college steals (**86**, 2008-2009)